What SEO Can't Do

By: Roggie Clark

Copyright

Title: What SEO Can't Do
Author: Roggie Clark

Cover Design: Roggie Clark
Editing: Renee' Clark

Printed in the United States of America

Disclaimer

The views and opinions expressed in this book are those of the author and do not necessarily reflect the official policy or position of any individual, company, or organization cited or referenced in the text.

The author is not affiliated with any of the individuals, companies, or organizations mentioned in the text, nor does the author receive any form of compensation for citing or referencing them. Some sample scenarios in this text are fictitious. Any similarity to actual persons, living or dead, is coincidental.

The professional information (strategies, tips, and concepts) in this text is distributed on an "as is" basis, without warranty. While every precaution has been taken in the preparation of the text to ensure all information is accurate, neither the author nor the publisher shall have any liability to any person or entity with respect to any loss or damage caused or alleged to be caused directly or indirectly by the instructions contained in this text or by the computer software and hardware products described in it.

Neither the author nor the publisher guarantees any specific results or outcomes, and the information provided in this text should not be construed as professional advice. Readers should always consult with a qualified professional before making any significant changes to their website or business.

By reading this text, you agree that the author nor the publisher is responsible for any direct, indirect, incidental, or consequential damages that may arise from the use of the information provided. You assume full responsibility for any actions taken based on the information presented in this text.

Table of Contents

Chapter 1: Introduction

SEO is often seen as a magic wand that can transform any business with a few well-placed keywords and a handful of backlinks. But in reality, SEO is a specialized field, requiring a blend of technical skills, strategic thinking, and ongoing optimization.

To be clear; An SEO specialist is a professional who improves a website's visibility in search engine results, driving traffic and supporting the site's overall goals. They work with search engine algorithms, on-page and off-page optimization, content strategy, and analytics, constantly analyzing and adjusting tactics to align with shifting industry standards. But while SEO specialists are skilled at increasing online visibility, their work has limits, especially when factors beyond their control come into play.

A common misconception is that an SEO specialist alone can drive all aspects of a business's success online. Many business owners believe SEOs are these "wizards" that can magically rescue a product or service struggling with deeper issues, such as poor quality or negative public perception. Some assume that SEO works instantly or that it can control how people respond to the brand. Others expect SEO to be a one-time fix that keeps results flowing indefinitely, or they mistakenly view SEO as an alternative to other marketing or customer service efforts. These assumptions create unrealistic expectations, leading to frustration when results don't meet them.

The truth is that SEO, while powerful, is not a cure-all. This book will delve into the many things that SEO cannot accomplish. From overcoming product flaws to solving economic downturns, SEO has its boundaries. For example, it "can't make a bad product good," nor can it "overcome a bad economy" or "fix internal company issues." It's not a substitute for high-quality customer service, other forms of marketing, or a well-functioning website. It also cannot guarantee results, control search engine algorithms, or provide immediate outcomes. These limitations are crucial for understanding the role of SEO within the broader marketing and business landscape.

In the chapters that follow, we'll explore each of these limits in detail, helping you as a reader better recognize where SEO can support your business goals and where it simply can not. By understanding these boundaries, business owners and marketers can better strategize, setting realistic expectations and incorporating SEO as one part of a larger, well-rounded marketing and business plan. Let's get started!

Chapter 2: Can't Make a Bad Product Good or Skew Poor Public Perception

One of the most common misconceptions about SEO is that it can fix a product that is inherently bad. While SEO can certainly drive traffic to a website, it cannot resolve fundamental issues with a product or service. If the product fails to meet customer expectations, no amount of SEO can salvage poor reviews or customer dissatisfaction.

During my time as an in-house SEO professional, I encountered a company where this was a significant problem. The company's external social media profiles were flooded with reviews mentioning how difficult the product was to use and how impossible it was to cancel. Despite this, the company's upper management seemed to ignore the feedback. It wasn't that they were unaware; they knew full well about the negative perception surrounding the product. In fact, I remember specifically telling them myself about the issues, but again the concerns were dismissed.

This is why money-driven behavior and SEO, or marketing in general, simply don't go together. SEO is not a magical solution that can bypass or conceal the real feelings customers have about your business. If they hate it, SEO ain't gonna change it. The truth is, many CEOs and upper management are so thin-skinned that they can't handle hearing negative feedback—whether it's from customers or their own team. Instead, they're often are willing to risk major consequences, like FTC violations, just to make a quick dollar.

This outdated mindset is one of the key reasons so many companies go bankrupt. They believe they can avoid hearing real feedback from customers and, instead, throw money into schemes like SEO to silence criticism. However, SEO cannot alter the public's perception or bypass customer dissatisfaction. The harsh reality is that many businesses hire SEO professionals with the false belief that SEO can fix these problems. News flash: it can't!

My advice to business owners is simple: take the time to understand your audience, listen to their feedback, and use that information to improve your product. You are in service to your customers, not the other way around. If you choose to ignore this advice, be aware that eventually, the consequences will catch up to you—whether on the front end or back end, you will feel the impact.

Chapter 3: Can't Overcome a Bad Economy

Since 2021, we've seen record-high inflation across the board—from everyday items like a loaf of bread to big-ticket purchases like homes and cars, and everything in between. Healthcare, childcare, gasoline, subscription services, pet food—the list goes on. Inflation has become rampant in the past four years, and to make matters worse, there has been a reluctance from presidential administrations and federal banking officials to stimulate the economy effectively, opting instead for a top-down, trickle-down approach.

We can speculate all day about the causes of this inflation and the ongoing deterioration of consumer spending, but let's get down to the basics: the U.S. dollar simply doesn't go as far as it used to. As a result, consumers are becoming increasingly picky about how and where they spend their money.

Additionally, they're more selective about doing business with companies that don't exhibit healthy business practices. The truth is, that trust in both businesses and the whole financial system as a whole has been eroded. Raising prices inexplicably or adding hidden fees will only further alienate customers.

In this new economic landscape, businesses must adapt in order to survive. SEO should no longer be seen as just a way to rank higher on Google or other search engines. Instead, think of SEO as a tool to gauge how customers truly feel about your business and an opportunity to build meaningful relationships. Don't be the company that cuts entire marketing teams just to meet arbitrary OKRs. Focus on allocating resources wisely because the era of perpetual stimulus and easy money, as we saw during the COVID-19 pandemic, is over. Businesses will only thrive based on what they have genuinely earned.

I've been hired many times by struggling businesses that are failing to adapt to the current economic climate. And without fail, I have to explain to executives what SEO can and can't do. This is where the concept of being an SEO evangelist comes into play—you are expected to make up for so many factors that SEO simply cannot influence. But the truth is, that's not my job anymore. I've put away that evangelist hat. It's not my responsibility to explain why the economy is in shambles; as a business owner, you need to do your research and recognize that the world is much bigger than your company. To succeed, you must act with that perspective in mind.

In a struggling economy, consumer spending patterns change drastically. SEO can't compel people to make purchases if they are financially constrained or unwilling to spend. While SEO can help maintain visibility, it can't override the broader economic challenges affecting purchasing power. Simply put, SEO can't fix a bad economy or solve systemic issues—it's a tool, not a magic bullet.

Chapter 4: Can't Fix Internal Company Issues

Too many CEOs believe they can get away with poor management practices, mistreating staff, and creating unnecessary work to justify their pay. They set meaningless deadlines, hold pointless meetings, and create mundane tasks just to feel like they're getting their "money's worth." This behavior is not only selfish and callous, but it also wastes valuable resources. It's one of the main reasons so many companies are failing.

These CEOs tend to blame their employees for poor performance, but in reality, employee behavior is simply a reflection of the toxic culture the leadership i.e. shareholders have fostered. If you regularly swindle people or treat them poorly, don't be surprised when your staff does the exact same.

SEO and other marketing efforts can't fix these internal issues. SEO amplifies what's already in place, for better or worse. If a company has unresolved issues like poor management, lack of communication, or inefficient processes, investing heavily in marketing won't solve the problem. In fact, it will only expose those flaws more widely. A business that fails to address its internal culture will struggle, no matter how much money it pours into advertising and branding.

I've worked in companies where more energy was spent monitoring employees than allowing actual work to happen. A common project that SEOs often handle is website redesigns or migrations, which are large and complex projects. These types of projects naturally stir up internal issues as employees start pointing fingers at each other over who is responsible for the website failing to be effective. But the truth is, a poorly managed website is usually just a reflection of the company's deeper problems. If the internal culture is toxic, it will manifest in every aspect of the business, including its digital presence.

I've never encountered a poorly executed website that didn't align with a company's overall dysfunction. The state of a company's website often mirrors the attitudes and behaviors within the organization. SEO professionals or any other marketing experts cannot fix these deep-rooted internal problems. No amount of strategy or optimization will work if the company's leadership doesn't make fundamental changes to the way it operates internally. Because what will happen is, if the SEO professional does implement meaningful changes, if the company is dysfunctional all these changes will eventually be erased.

My advice is simple: slow down. Take a long, hard look at your business culture. Would you want to work for your company? If you can't stand yourself or the way your business operates, don't expect others to. Before you invest in SEO or any other marketing efforts, address the internal issues that are holding you back. Fix those first, and the rest will follow.

Chapter 5: Can't Run on Autopilot

I really wish SEO professionals would stop telling business owners that SEO is a set-it-and-forget-it strategy —because it's not, by a long shot. SEO requires constant attention, updates, and adaptation to changes in algorithms and market trends. It demands continuous monitoring, analysis, and tweaking to stay effective.

In the time it takes you to read this book, search engines may have changed their algorithm nearly a hundred times. It's truly a cat-and-mouse game, which is why I don't recommend rushing into SEO. Instead, I encourage people to think of SEO as a long-term part of their business strategy. Stop being in such a rush to fire your marketing team—business will always need marketing. If you decide to invest in SEO, do it for the long haul. Don't expect to get some quick fix or "guru secret" that will instantly solve everything.

I've seen this many times from CEOs and even employees when they've had me interview with them. Their faces light up when I explain how I do SEO, and they often try to be clever by asking me to share my strategies or "secret sauce." I can't help but laugh at them because SEO isn't rocket science, and there's no "secret sauce." All my strategies and tactics are well-researched and easy to find online. What these companies are hoping to avoid is long-term accountability and streamlined success without putting in the real work.

They think that because they went down to the bank and got a loan, they're somehow special. But they're not. This is why, in the past four years, so many terrible companies have emerged that lack basic business acumen and structure. It's time to retire the words "passive income" because they encourage wasteful, ill-advised business practices. There's no such thing, and SEO is no different.

My advice is simple: find a good SEO professional, and be prepared to work with them for the long haul. SEO isn't a one-time fix—it's an ongoing commitment.

Chapter 6: Can't Be Used as a Substitute for Other Marketing Efforts

While SEO is undeniably important, it is not an all-encompassing strategy. In other words, SEO is not a replacement for traditional marketing efforts like print media, radio, or television. It also does not substitute for other digital marketing channels such as social media, email marketing, or paid advertising. Instead, SEO should work in harmony with these other forms of marketing to create a well-rounded strategy.

A common mistake among businesses is the belief that once SEO is optimized, they can simply eliminate other marketing efforts. This is a shortsighted approach that often leads to frustration and failure. It's an example of ill-advised business practices—one that assumes SEO alone can drive all the growth and visibility a business needs. In reality, no single marketing channel can achieve everything on its own, and SEO is no exception. It is crucial that businesses continue to invest in other marketing initiatives even as they optimize for search engines.

Furthermore, some companies make the mistake of overloading their marketing teams once SEO is in place. They think that because SEO is effective, it will replace the need for other specialists, or they force their SEO experts to take on additional marketing responsibilities. This often results in diminishing returns. It's more productive to let each expert focus on what they do best rather than overloading them with tasks outside their core competency. The idea of the "Swiss army knife" employee, who is expected to juggle multiple marketing functions, is outdated and counterproductive. Overloading your team can lead to burnout, a drop in quality, and an increase in turnover.

The concept of "bandwidth" is frequently discussed in corporate environments, and for good reason. Many employees are stretched too thin as they try to manage multiple roles. For businesses, this is not just inefficient; it's costly. Rather than expecting employees to wear many hats, businesses should prioritize creating dedicated teams for each marketing function. By investing in specialists, companies can ensure that each area of marketing—SEO, social media, content creation, etc.—gets the attention it deserves.

My best advice for businesses is to think long-term and invest in a robust marketing team, including dedicated SEO specialists. This approach leads to better results, less employee burnout, and ultimately, a stronger, more cohesive marketing strategy. While it's fine to seek input from experts across disciplines, expecting one person to handle everything will likely lead to failure. It's crucial to keep SEO as part of a larger marketing ecosystem, where it can support, rather than replace, other efforts.

Chapter 7: Can't Be a Solution to Low Capital Expenditure

I'm not going to blame you for thinking that SEO is free. Why? Because so many irresponsible SEO specialists have marketed it this way, selling companies on the idea of "free" SEO just to make a quick buck. We all have to eat, but this should never come at the expense of honesty or integrity. That's why I never tell clients that SEO is a one-time, set-it-and-forget-it solution. An effective SEO strategy requires a serious investment of time, tools, resources, and skilled professionals. While SEO can be cost-effective in the long term, the initial implementation can require a financial commitment that low capital simply cannot support.

The misconception that SEO is "free" often leads companies to undervalue the expertise needed to make it successful. But this is a mistake. Proper SEO requires access to the right tools, which come with a cost. From keyword research platforms to analytics software and link-building tools, these are not freebies. Additionally, SEO professionals need to stay up-to-date on the latest trends, algorithm updates, and best practices—investments that pay off when used effectively. The idea that SEO can be executed without financial commitment is simply unrealistic.

So, how much should you expect to pay for SEO services? The cost can vary, but generally, you can expect to pay anywhere from $20 to $100 per hour for a competent SEO professional. This equates to anywhere from $1,000 to $10,000 per month, depending on the scope of work. Prices may fluctuate depending on the complexity of the project, the industry, and the professional's experience. However, the key point is this: SEO is an investment. The earlier you recognize that, the better prepared you'll be to choose the right SEO partner for your business.

When looking to hire an SEO professional, it's important to vet them thoroughly. A good starting point is to ask questions like: "What types of clients have you worked with?" "How do you stay updated on SEO trends?" and "Can you provide case studies or samples of previous projects?" These questions are crucial because they help ensure you're hiring someone with the expertise and experience necessary to handle your SEO needs. Don't rush into hiring someone just because you're in a hurry to fill the position. Take the time to evaluate their fit for your company. Better to start with a small project and validate their work before making a long-term commitment.

It's understandable why many companies are hesitant to invest in SEO—they've likely been burned by inexperienced SEO professionals in the past. However, that problem can often be avoided with proper vetting. If you've been burned before, take this lesson to heart: do your research, ask the right questions, and start with a small project. It may take a little more time, but the results will be worth the investment. Trust me, it's far better than rushing into a long-term commitment that ends up costing more in the long run. Got it?

Chapter 8: Can't Be Substituted for a Poor Website Experience

A common mistake many businesses make is hiring an SEO specialist before their website is at a baseline level of usability. Similarly, when redesigning a site, SEO is sometimes excluded from the process entirely. This can lead to frustration, as business owners often wonder why their site isn't converting or why their SEO expert isn't performing as expected. The truth is, that SEO specialists are not responsible for making your website visually appealing or highly functional. Their primary job is to drive traffic to your website, not to ensure those visitors become customers.

To build a successful website, it's crucial to invest time in hiring a qualified web developer. They can create an aesthetically pleasing, user-friendly website that complements your SEO efforts. Additionally, researching other websites that are performing well in your industry can provide valuable insights into what works and what doesn't. By studying these successful examples, you can incorporate design elements and features that will help optimize your site for conversions.

So, how can you tell if your website is struggling? Here are a few telltale signs of a poor user experience: If it takes more than three clicks to find key information, if it takes more than three seconds to load, or if the colors and fonts are difficult to read or clash with each other, you likely have a subpar site. These are just a few of the most common issues, but the underlying message is clear—your website should not make it difficult for users to make a purchase or schedule an appointment, especially if you're in a service-based industry.

An essential component of a website's success is its usability. SEO can bring visitors to your site, but if your website is slow, cluttered, or difficult to navigate, these visitors will leave quickly. Users expect fast loading times, intuitive navigation, and a pleasant visual experience. If your site doesn't meet these expectations, even the best SEO strategy won't help retain visitors or convert them into loyal customers.

Involving an SEO specialist early in the website design and development process can help avoid many of these pitfalls. A properly designed site, optimized for speed and usability, will ensure that the traffic brought in through SEO efforts will have a seamless experience. Ultimately, this will increase your chances of converting those visitors into customers, whether you're selling products or offering services.

Chapter 9: Can't Provide Guaranteed or Immediate Results

SEO is not a guaranteed or immediate solution. Just because you invest in a specialist, tools, or other resources, doesn't mean you'll see instant results. It's not as simple as paying for SEO and then watching droves of customers flood your website overnight. If it were that easy, everyone would be doing it and reaping the rewards right away. But the reality is that, like most things in life, SEO takes time and effort to produce meaningful results.

Think about it: is there anything in life that's guaranteed to be fast and easy? Most successful endeavors —whether building a career, growing a business, or achieving personal goals—require patience and perseverance. SEO is no different. It demands long-term commitment, continuous effort, and, above all, patience. It's about staying the course, even when things feel slow or uncertain.

However, the SEO specialist you work with should still be actively doing their job to ensure that progress is being made. Like I said earlier, this is why properly vetting your SEO provider is crucial. When you've done your research and selected the right professional, you'll know whether you're facing the natural challenges of SEO or if you're being misled.

It’s important to understand that SEO specialists have limited control over the search engines they’re optimizing your website for. Search engines like Google continually update and tweak their algorithms to improve the quality of search results. These changes can happen frequently—sometimes hundreds of times in a year. In fact, it has been reported that Google could change its algorithm more than 3,000 times annually. This means that what works well today might not be effective tomorrow. SEO specialists can’t predict these changes or guarantee how they’ll affect rankings, which is why SEO is always a bit of a moving target.

This constant evolution of search engine algorithms reinforces why SEO cannot be a set-it-and-forget-it strategy. SEO requires ongoing attention and adjustments. If your website starts to drop in rankings after a new algorithm update, your SEO specialist needs to adapt your strategy to account for those changes. If you stop investing in SEO, your progress could stall, and your website might lose its competitive edge. SEO is a long-term game, and without consistent investment, the benefits can quickly fade away.

In conclusion, SEO should not be treated as a quick fix or a surefire guarantee for immediate success. It’s a complex, ever-changing process that requires careful planning, ongoing investment, and a great deal of patience. While there’s no way to predict the future of search engine rankings with certainty, working with a qualified SEO professional who understands these dynamics can help you navigate the journey and avoid unnecessary setbacks. But remember: the key to success in SEO is understanding that results take time—and that nothing worthwhile happens overnight.

Chapter 10: Can't Be Mastered Quickly

If you're planning on doing SEO yourself, it's important to understand that mastering SEO—whether it's the basics or advanced strategies—cannot happen overnight. While you can certainly pick up a lot of information quickly, SEO is not a skill that can be mastered in a single day. The learning process takes time, and it's important to approach SEO with the mindset that it's a long-term endeavor, not a quick-fix solution. SEO is a complex field that is constantly evolving with new trends, algorithm updates, and changing user behaviors. As such, it's not something that can be fully understood or implemented within 24 hours.

This is why I emphasize the importance of treating SEO as a *slow-burn strategy*. Mastering SEO requires dedication and a commitment to continuous learning. What you learn today may evolve tomorrow, and you'll need to stay updated on the latest changes to search engine algorithms and best practices. Whether you're optimizing for better rankings or improving user experience, SEO will require ongoing adaptation and flexibility. Understanding this fundamental truth will help you avoid the frustration of expecting immediate results and allow you to build a more sustainable and long-term SEO strategy.

For those starting out, my best advice is to focus on the fundamentals. SEO may seem overwhelming at first, but you can break it down into manageable parts. Begin by learning the basics, such as understanding how search engines work, the importance of **keyword research**, **on-page SEO techniques**, **off-page SEO strategies**, and **technical SEO**. Each of these areas contributes to the larger picture of SEO success, and mastering them one at a time will make the learning process more digestible. Don't try to learn everything at once; instead, build your knowledge incrementally.

One of the most crucial parts of learning SEO is actually implementing what you've learned. Don't just read articles and watch tutorials—put your knowledge into practice. Start small with personal projects or test websites where you can apply different SEO techniques and track their performance. This hands-on approach will give you a clearer understanding of how SEO works in real-world scenarios and help solidify the concepts you're learning. By experimenting with real data, you'll also begin to see firsthand how small changes can impact your website's performance.

If you're serious about mastering SEO but find yourself struggling or feeling overwhelmed, there's absolutely no harm in seeking external help. Consider bringing in an SEO expert as a coach to guide you and review your work. Hiring a coach or consultant might involve a small financial investment, but it can pay off in the long run. A seasoned professional can provide you with tailored feedback, help you avoid common pitfalls, and offer strategic insights that might otherwise take you years to discover on your own. SEO is a continuously evolving field, and learning from someone who's already navigated its complexities can accelerate your growth and ensure you're on the right track.

Chapter 11: Can't Eliminate Competition

No matter what an SEO professional might tell you, implementing SEO on your website, no matter how well you do it, will not eliminate your competition. There are a few obvious reasons for this.

First and foremost, your competitors are likely investing in SEO as well, just like you. They are actively working to improve their visibility on search engines and targeting the same audience as you are. SEO is all about improving your website's ranking, but by design, search engine results are competitive. Every page that ranks highly has likely gone through some level of optimization, making it a battle for position on the search engine results pages (SERPs). In other words, SEO doesn't guarantee that your website will "destroy" your competition—search engine platforms are neutral, and they don't take sides.

I often find myself explaining this to clients who become frustrated when their competitors rank just below them or seem to have a slight edge. They might wonder, "Why isn't my website always at the top?" or "Why am I not beating my competitors if I'm doing everything right?" The reality is that SEO isn't about eliminating the competition; it's about doing your best to rank highly on your own terms. There will always be competition on the SERPs because that's how the system works. What you can control is how well you optimize your own website and the content you offer to users.

In fact, SEO can help you become more competitive with your competition. One of the key strategies in SEO is competitor analysis. This process involves studying your competitors to see what they're doing right (or wrong) so you can find opportunities to outrank them. By analyzing their keyword strategy, backlinks, content quality, and user experience, you can gain valuable insights into how to improve your own site and compete more effectively. This kind of strategic planning allows you to adjust your own approach and create a more targeted, informed SEO strategy.

However, even with thorough competitor analysis and excellent SEO practices, completely eliminating competition from search results isn't realistic. The reality is that there will always be others competing for similar keywords, and some will always have an advantage due to factors beyond SEO, such as brand recognition, existing authority in the market, or greater financial resources for ongoing optimization. SEO is a long-term effort, and there will always be fluctuation in rankings, with some competitors gaining ground and others falling behind.

In conclusion, while SEO is an incredibly powerful tool for improving your website's visibility and competitiveness, it's important to set realistic expectations. SEO isn't a magic bullet that will eliminate competition; rather, it's a way to level the playing field and improve your chances of outranking others. Focus on creating a strong, competitive presence in your market, and remember that SEO is a long-term investment in growing your business—one that requires ongoing effort and adaptation to stay ahead of the curve.

Chapter 12: Can't Bypass Legal Issues or Privacy Laws

When engaging in content creation, it's natural to want to create SEO content that has the potential to go viral or rank highly. However, not every SEO content idea is safe or legally appropriate to execute. In the realm of SEO, there are legal issues and privacy laws that must be considered. SEO cannot bypass these regulations because they are designed to protect users' rights and ensure a fair and transparent online environment. Laws such as the **General Data Protection Regulation (GDPR)** in the European Union and the **California Consumer Privacy Act (CCPA)** in the United States govern how user data is collected, stored, and used. These legal frameworks aim to give users control over their personal information and prevent exploitation by businesses.

As an SEO professional, it's essential to operate within these legal boundaries, as failing to do so can result in severe consequences, including hefty fines and damage to a company's reputation. Violating privacy laws can not only bring legal action against a business but also lead to a loss of consumer trust, which is far more damaging in the long run than any temporary SEO success. It's important to recognize that SEO strategies focused solely on rankings, without regard to legal and ethical considerations, can backfire. Engaging in tactics that violate legal standards can result in lawsuits, penalties, and long-term harm to a business's online presence and credibility.

During my time as an SEO manager at a corporation, I witnessed firsthand how SEO content creation could run into legal troubles. For example, there were instances where we wanted to compare our services to those of our competitors. We aimed to highlight the advantages of our offerings, showing the pros and cons of each, and explain why our company was the better choice. While competitive content is often a valuable business practice, it is essential to be cautious about the claims made in such content.

In our case, we faced several cease-and-desist letters from one of our competitors due to the claims we made about their products. While this didn't escalate into a major legal battle, it did serve as a critical reminder of the importance of being mindful about what content is published, even when it's meant to highlight your company's strengths. This experience reinforced the need to create content that is both legally compliant and mindful of competitors' reputations.

In addition to the legal considerations surrounding content creation, privacy laws play a significant role in how SEO strategies can be implemented. As I said, privacy laws like the GDPR and CCPA place strict limitations on how personal data can be used. SEO often involves collecting and analyzing user data to better optimize content, personalize user experiences, and improve website performance. However, these activities must be done in strict accordance with the law. Data tracking, for example, must be transparent, and users must be informed of how their information is being used, with clear options for consent. Attempting to bypass these consent requirements or using personal data without permission, again, can lead to serious repercussions, both legally and ethically.

Ultimately, SEO must strike a balance between optimization and respect for privacy. While the use of data analytics to refine content strategies is vital for improving performance, it cannot come at the cost of violating privacy regulations. The key to building long-term success in SEO is not just about leveraging the latest techniques or driving up rankings; it's about doing so in a way that fosters trust, aligns with legal standards, and ensures a positive user experience.

Businesses that prioritize compliance with privacy laws and create ethical, user-first content are far more likely to build a sustainable online presence that resonates with both users and search engines alike.

Chapter 13: Can't Control External Websites and Businesses

Again, I don't care what other SEO professional tells you, contrary to popular belief; SEO cannot influence how other websites or businesses behave, particularly when it comes to backlinks, competitor strategies, and online presence. While SEO professionals can control what happens within the boundaries of the website they're optimizing, they have no authority over external sites and their activities. These factors must be managed through strategic relationships, partnerships, and ongoing engagement, rather than relying solely on SEO efforts.

Like I said, one of the key limitations SEO professionals face is the inability to control external websites, especially those hosting valuable backlinks. These sites operate independently, with their own set of rules, objectives, and maintenance schedules. As such, SEO experts cannot dictate when or if these external sites will provide a link back, whether they will maintain the link over time, or how they will present the linked content. Changes like broken links, content alterations, or the removal of entire pages on external sites are beyond the control of SEO practitioners, making it challenging to depend on these external sources for sustained ranking improvements.

In addition, businesses within the same industry or niche can independently make decisions that directly impact search engine results and your website’s SEO performance. Competitors may launch new marketing campaigns, target different keywords, or adjust their content strategies, which can shift the competitive landscape and affect rankings. Search engines regularly update their algorithms, and these updates consider a variety of external factors, including how businesses within the same sector operate online. As a result, SEO professionals must continuously monitor competitors and adjust their own strategies, but they cannot predict or control their competitors’ actions.

As I said in Chapter 2; SEO professionals also encounter limitations when attempting to influence external platforms like social media, review sites, and forums. These platforms often play a crucial role in enhancing online visibility and reputation, yet their algorithms, user engagement rules, and content guidelines are entirely out of the SEO professional's hands.

Negative reviews, poor user engagement, or unfavorable mentions on third-party platforms can harm your online reputation and affect search rankings. While SEO can include reputation management techniques, such as addressing negative reviews or boosting positive mentions, it cannot guarantee control over how these platforms display content, interact with users, or prioritize your brand.

This lack of control over external factors underscores the importance of focusing on what SEO professionals can directly influence—optimizing on-site content, technical performance, and user experience. A comprehensive SEO strategy must include proactive on-page optimization, ensuring the website is consistently well-maintained and performs effectively. Ultimately, while SEO can improve rankings by optimizing a site's internal components and monitoring external factors, the unpredictable nature of external websites and competitor behavior highlights the need for adaptability, resilience, and a balanced approach in the ever-changing world of digital marketing.

Chapter 14: Can't Ensure Guaranteed Customer Loyalty or Sales

While SEO is an essential tool for attracting visitors to a website, it cannot guarantee customer buy-in, loyalty, or sales. The primary role of SEO is to enhance a site's visibility on search engines, ensuring that potential customers can easily discover it when they search for relevant topics. SEO can drive a substantial amount of traffic, but simply bringing people to your site is not enough to ensure they will engage with your brand or make a purchase. The days of just pumping out content and building a lazy funnel are over, now the journey from a click to a loyal customer involves much more than being discovered—it requires building a connection, trust, and offering a compelling reason for visitors to return.

SEO is designed to improve the discoverability of a site, making it easier for users to find relevant content and solutions. However, customer buy-in and loyalty are influenced by deeper, more personal factors than SEO can address. These factors include the customer experience, the trustworthiness of the brand, and the emotional connection fostered over time. While SEO-optimized content can provide valuable information and showcase expertise, it cannot establish the rapport and trust necessary for long-term customer relationships. This trust is built through consistent interactions, quality service, and a clear demonstration of the brand's values and authenticity.

Again like I said in Chapter 2, SEO does not address key aspects that contribute to customer loyalty and sales, such as product quality, pricing, and customer service. Even if a website ranks highly on search engines, customers may still choose to leave without purchasing if the products or services do not meet their expectations. For instance, if the prices are too high or if the product offerings do not match their needs, customers may not convert despite high visibility. In other words, SEO can guide customers to the door, but the business must deliver on its promises to convert visitors into loyal customers.

A customer's journey from discovering a brand to making a purchase involves multiple touchpoints, such as social media engagement, email marketing, and interactions with customer support. SEO can certainly attract users, but these other elements are just as crucial in building lasting relationships. A website must be designed to provide a seamless, informative, and engaging experience that resonates with users' needs and expectations. If the website is difficult to navigate or lacks the information a visitor is looking for, even the most optimized SEO efforts will fail to convert visitors into customers.

Companies need to invest in holistic marketing strategies that nurture customer relationships over time, including personalized marketing, customer service excellence, and loyalty programs. These strategies are vital for fostering brand loyalty, something SEO alone cannot achieve. In essence, SEO plays an important role in driving visibility and traffic, but it is only one piece of a broader marketing strategy aimed at creating lasting customer loyalty and sustained sales.

Chapter 15: Can't Replace Building a Strong Brand

While SEO is undoubtedly an essential tool for driving online visibility, it cannot replace the critical need for building a strong, recognizable brand. Again, SEO's primary function is to optimize content in alignment with search engine algorithms, improve rankings, and target relevant keywords. These tactics are designed to boost discoverability, but they focus more on attracting traffic rather than creating an emotional connection or fostering long-term customer loyalty. At its core, SEO is about visibility, not identity—something that a strong brand must establish.

Branding, on the other hand, encompasses much more than just getting noticed. It involves creating a unique value proposition, defining a distinctive brand voice, and establishing emotional connections with an audience. While SEO can help users find a business, it cannot build the trust or loyalty that a strong brand fosters. A brand is what resonates with customers on a deeper level, communicating not just what a business does, but who they are, what they stand for, and why they matter. A business with a defined brand creates a sense of belonging that makes customers feel like they are part of something larger than just a transaction.

A strong brand is what differentiates a business in a crowded marketplace. It goes beyond the mechanics of search engine algorithms to create an identity that is memorable and easily recognizable. This includes visual elements like logos, color schemes, and typography, as well as messaging through slogans and taglines.

Again like I said in Chapter 14, SEO can bring visitors to your website, but without a clear, compelling brand narrative, those visitors may leave without truly understanding what makes your business unique. Without a strong brand identity, even a high-ranking website may struggle to convert traffic into loyal customers. Branding builds emotional resonance, which SEO cannot achieve on its own.

Moreover, a strong brand leads to opportunities for organic growth that go far beyond search engine rankings. A business with a solid brand enjoys customer advocacy, word-of-mouth marketing, and organic engagement—all of which contribute to sustainable growth. Loyal customers are more likely to share their positive experiences, recommend products, and engage with the brand on social media. This type of growth is not dependent on keyword strategies or algorithm updates but on the trust and emotional connections that a brand creates. SEO can bring users to a website, but it is the brand experience that keeps them coming back.

While SEO is an invaluable tool for improving visibility and attracting traffic, it cannot replace the importance of developing a strong, authentic brand. SEO may help you get noticed, but it's your brand that will make a lasting impression and convert casual visitors into loyal advocates. A compelling brand ensures long-term success, driving growth and loyalty in ways that SEO alone simply cannot achieve. Therefore, SEO should be viewed as a complementary strategy—one that supports and enhances the power of a well-established brand.

Chapter 16: Can't Create Demand for a Non-Existent Market

SEO (Search Engine Optimization) is an incredibly powerful tool for capturing demand that already exists. However, it cannot create demand where none is present. SEO operates by optimizing content to match the search queries that people are already making, based on their existing interests or needs.

For SEO to be effective, there must be a baseline level of established interest in the product, service, or information being offered. If a business is attempting to introduce an entirely new product or service to a market where no demand currently exists, SEO alone will struggle to generate meaningful interest. This is because, in the absence of search traffic or search intent, people aren't actively looking for the solution being provided, making SEO a less viable tool for market creation.

When a business tries to introduce an innovative product or break into a market that doesn't yet have a developed consumer base, SEO won't be able to attract customers who don't yet recognize the need for the offering. For example, if a product solves a problem that no one yet knows they have, SEO's primary role—matching keywords with existing search queries—becomes irrelevant. Without search volume or interest, targeting keywords and improving search visibility won't generate the demand necessary to drive traffic. In these situations, SEO can only be effective once the market begins to evolve, and potential customers start actively seeking out the solution.

Again, during my time as an in-house SEO professional, I encountered this, where the company I was working for was attempting to launch a new product but hadn't taken the time first to see if any demand existed. In order to get some type of traffic I had to amalgamate different keywords. Looking back, this honestly didn't work, because the web content I created was not specifically applicable/targeted to the keywords I was using. So again it is highly critical to do research first and then do product creation second.

Creating demand for a non-existent market is a complex process that extends far beyond the reach of SEO. It requires proactive efforts to educate potential customers, raise awareness, and spark curiosity. These tasks often require traditional marketing methods such as content marketing, social media outreach, public relations campaigns, and influencer collaborations.

These strategies are essential for introducing new ideas to the audience, helping them understand how the product can fit into their lives, and demonstrating its unique value proposition. Only through these efforts can a brand build the kind of awareness and interest needed to cultivate a new market. Once people start recognizing the need for the product or service, they may then turn to search engines to learn more, at which point SEO can play a valuable role in directing traffic and capturing this growing demand.

Even once people become aware of a new product through these external channels, SEO alone cannot fully educate or persuade them to take action. Demand creation often involves a combination of storytelling, emotional engagement, and trust-building—elements that are better achieved through advertising, personal brand engagement, and a comprehensive approach to marketing across multiple platforms.

It’s not enough for potential customers to know the product exists; they need to be convinced that it will solve a problem or fulfill a need in a way that nothing else can. SEO is not designed for this kind of persuasive engagement. It’s a reactive tool that capitalizes on demand that has already been created through other means. For businesses entering entirely new or untested markets, SEO must play a supporting role in capturing demand once it's been generated by other efforts.

SEO cannot be relied upon as a standalone strategy for creating demand for a non-existent market. For businesses introducing innovative products, a comprehensive marketing strategy that combines SEO with brand-building initiatives, awareness campaigns, and educational content is critical. SEO should be part of a broader, integrated marketing approach, one that positions the brand as a solution to an emerging need, nurtures interest, and supports the eventual growth of organic demand. Only when awareness, trust, and customer interest have been established can SEO truly unlock its full potential in driving traffic and growing the business.

Chapter 17: Can't Replace Expertise, Insights, or Human Creativity

While SEO is an invaluable tool for optimizing digital content and reaching target audiences, it cannot replace the depth and nuance that human expertise brings to the table. Search engines rely on complex algorithms that evaluate factors such as keywords, backlinks, and technical aspects of a website, but these metrics only measure certain elements of value.

True expertise, on the other hand, is built on a foundation of experience, specialized knowledge, and an understanding of industry-specific subtleties that SEO alone cannot capture. For instance, an experienced professional in a particular field can provide insights that extend far beyond keyword-based content. These insights add real value to readers that SEO alone simply cannot achieve, as it overlooks the intricate knowledge that comes from hands-on experience and a deeper understanding of the subject matter.

Beyond just expertise, SEO also falls short when it comes to replicating human insights. Search engines assess content based on patterns, but they miss the richness that comes from human intuition and contextual awareness. Content creators with deep industry knowledge can address unique audience needs, explore complex topics, and adapt content to fit current trends, cultural nuances, and emotional factors. SEO-driven content, while helpful in ensuring visibility, lacks the understanding that humans possess about what truly resonates with audiences. Only through human insights can content evolve from being informative to being deeply engaging, offering a level of relevance and emotional connection that algorithms can't replicate.

Another critical area where SEO cannot match human capability is creativity. Creativity is an inherently human quality that search engines simply cannot automate. SEO strategies can suggest how content should be structured or provide insights into popular topics, but they cannot innovate or create original ideas.

True creativity goes beyond formulaic content; it involves storytelling, innovation, and developing unique approaches that differentiate a brand in a crowded digital space. When content is driven purely by SEO tactics, there's a risk of it becoming repetitive and predictable. It's the creative minds behind content that breathe life into it, making it stand out from the crowd and ensuring it leaves a lasting impression on audiences.

Moreover, human creativity is what fuels the unique voice of a brand. SEO can help content appear in search results, but it doesn't shape the tone, personality, or narrative that makes content memorable. Great content isn't just about being found; it's about being valued and remembered. Creative content that taps into emotions, tells a compelling story, or offers something new can spark conversations and drive deeper engagement. Without human creativity, content risks becoming sterile and forgettable, merely ticking the boxes required by search algorithms. It's this combination of SEO's technical guidance and human creativity that makes content not just visible, but impactful.

Again, while SEO is an essential component of a successful digital marketing strategy, it cannot replace the value that expertise, insights, and creativity bring to content creation. Expertise ensures content is accurate and valuable; human insights allow it to resonate on a deeper level with audiences, and creativity ensures it stands out from the crowd. By blending SEO with human ingenuity, content can achieve both visibility and relevance, ensuring it is not only discoverable but also meaningful. SEO may help amplify content, but it is the human touch that truly makes content memorable and impactful.

Chapter 18: Can't Work Without a Plan and Strategy

SEO is a complex, multifaceted discipline that requires careful planning and strategic thinking to achieve sustainable, long-term results. Without a clear plan in place, SEO efforts can easily become scattered and ineffective. It's common to overlook critical components like keyword targeting, content quality, and technical optimization when there is no strategy guiding these efforts. A well-defined SEO strategy is essential because it establishes clear, actionable goals, ensuring that SEO activities directly align with broader business objectives. For example, focusing on increasing organic traffic, generating leads, or improving conversion rates helps SEO professionals prioritize tasks that will make the most significant impact.

A structured SEO strategy is especially important because SEO is a long-term commitment. Success doesn't come overnight, and consistent, cumulative efforts are necessary across various areas, such as content creation, link building, and on-page optimization. Without a strategic roadmap, there's a risk of neglecting one aspect in favor of another, or focusing on short-term tactics that deliver quick wins but fail to create sustainable value.

A clear plan helps SEO practitioners maintain a balanced approach, ensuring that all efforts contribute to the bigger picture. For instance, focusing on high-intent keywords initially, followed by a shift to long-tail keywords for sustained growth, is a tactic that a comprehensive plan ensures is carried out effectively over time.

Another critical benefit of an SEO strategy is its ability to guide decisions during times of change. SEO is an ever-evolving field, with search engine algorithms regularly updated to improve user experience and refine how content is ranked. These shifts can significantly impact rankings and traffic if SEO professionals are unprepared. A strategy provides the flexibility to adapt and respond to changes proactively rather than reactively. Whether this means investing more in high-quality content, technical SEO improvements, or a different approach to link building, having a well-thought-out plan helps ensure that SEO efforts remain relevant and effective, even as the digital landscape evolves.

SEO without a plan can easily result in missed opportunities. Without clearly defined goals and priorities, SEO efforts may become aimless, leading to wasted time, resources, and missed chances to optimize for the right keywords or target the right audience. A strategic approach allows SEO professionals to evaluate progress regularly, assess what's working and what's not, and make necessary adjustments. This ongoing evaluation is key to ensuring that SEO campaigns remain focused on achieving tangible business outcomes, rather than just driving traffic for the sake of traffic.

Like I said in Chapter 4, SEO is not a "set-it-and-forget-it" effort. It requires a thoughtful, ongoing strategy that adapts to changes in both search engine algorithms and user behavior. Without a plan, SEO efforts lack direction, making it difficult to achieve and sustain high search rankings and valuable organic traffic. A strategic framework ensures that all actions align with the overall business goals, prioritize the most effective tactics, and help SEO professionals navigate the long-term, evolving nature of search engine optimization. Only with a solid strategy in place can SEO deliver consistent, measurable results that truly benefit a business in the competitive online space.

Last Thoughts

As we conclude this exploration into the limitations of SEO, it's important to recognize that understanding what SEO can't do is just as crucial as knowing what it can do. Armed with this knowledge, you now have a clearer perspective on how SEO should fit into your overall strategy. SEO is not a magic fix or a standalone solution; it is a powerful tool when applied within a comprehensive, well-rounded business plan. So, what can you do now that you have a better understanding of SEO's boundaries?

First, focus on the elements of your business or website that are within your control. While SEO can help bring traffic, it can't fix fundamental issues such as poor product quality, negative public perception, or a flawed user experience. Ensure that the core of your business is solid—deliver quality, create a strong brand, and prioritize customer satisfaction. SEO can amplify your efforts, but it cannot make up for a subpar offering. If you haven't already, use the insights from this book to audit your product or service offerings and your brand perception in the market.

Next, use SEO to complement, not replace, other marketing efforts. I've emphasized that SEO cannot replace the need for a robust social media presence, a solid content marketing strategy, or even traditional advertising. You can now see how SEO works best when integrated with other strategies. For example, while SEO brings in organic traffic, your email marketing campaigns, social media ads, and influencer partnerships can help convert that traffic into loyal customers. Consider SEO as part of a larger, interwoven strategy that brings synergy to all your marketing channels.

It’s also vital that you recognize SEO is not a "set it and forget it" tactic. As you now know, SEO requires ongoing effort and optimization. This means continuous content creation, regular technical updates, and staying informed on the ever-changing algorithms that affect search rankings. You can’t simply rely on initial optimization to sustain your position—SEO is an evolving practice that demands constant attention. This understanding can help you develop a sustainable approach, ensuring you stay competitive in a fast-paced digital landscape.

In addition, understanding SEO’s limitations can guide you to avoid unrealistic expectations. SEO cannot guarantee instant results, nor can it promise to eliminate competition. This can save you time, money, and frustration. It’s important to manage expectations with clients or within your own organization. Instead of expecting immediate traffic surges or rankings that suddenly skyrocket, focus on the long-term process. View SEO as a gradual journey that builds cumulative results over time, rather than a quick fix for instant success.

Finally, with the knowledge of what SEO can’t do, you are now in a position to think more strategically about how to invest your resources. SEO can be an essential part of your digital growth, but it's not the end-all solution. Leverage what you've learned to make smarter decisions on where to allocate your budget and focus efforts. For example, while SEO might not be able to create demand for a non-existent market, it can help position you within an existing demand. Again, use the insights from this book to shape your approach to SEO and to ensure it aligns with your overall business goals.

In conclusion, understanding SEO's limitations allows you to approach it with a balanced mindset. Armed with these insights, you're ready to take SEO's strengths and apply them where they matter most. It's not a tool for instant results or magical fixes, but with strategic use, it can be a powerful ally in driving organic growth and long-term success.

Thank you for reading this book, and I wish you the best of luck on your SEO journey! Whether you take it on yourself or work with an expert, remember that the key to success lies in continuous learning, adaptability, and a clear vision for your digital presence.

About the Author

Roggie (Raj) Clark, is a 9 year SEO professional and owner of the SEO agency; *Bounce Rank.* Prior to joining the SEO industry, Raj was a web developer and school teacher. It was through creating his own websites, and wanting a career change from teaching, that Raj stumbled across the world of SEO.

Since joining the field nearly a decade ago, Raj has worked on a wide range of campaigns, from eCommerce, to B2B, to Healthcare, for enterprise companies and marketing agencies in the United States.

He is regarded as an expert, and guru by his colleagues, and the SEO industry. Raj currently lives in Maryland with his sister and niece.

www.ingramcontent.com/pod-product-compliance
Lightning Source LLC
LaVergne TN
LVHW022321200926
848481LV00004B/1395
9798295545252